# STORIES
# TO SOLVE

# STORIES TO SOLVE

## Folktales from Around the World

TOLD BY

### George Shannon

ILLUSTRATED BY

### Peter Sis

A TRUMPET CLUB SPECIAL EDITION

Published by The Trumpet Club
666 Fifth Avenue, New York, New York 10103

Text copyright © 1985 by George W.B. Shannon
Illustrations copyright © 1985 by Peter Sis

ISBN: 0-440-84396-0

This edition published by arrangement with Greenwillow Books,
a division of William Morrow & Company, Inc.
Printed in the United States of America
September 1991

10 9 8 7 6 5 4 3

CW

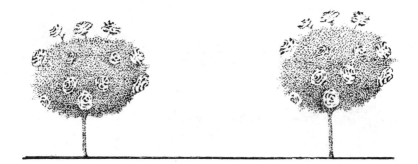

*TO ALL WHO*
*HEARD THESE TALES*
*AND PASSED THEM ON,*
*ALLOWING ME*
*TO SHARE THEM NOW*

—*G. S.*

*TO MY MOTHER*

—*P. S.*

# CONTENTS

# INTRODUCTION

Stories and mysteries have existed as long as there have been people to tell them and question why. The following folktales each involve a mystery or problem to be solved by the story's characters. And then, in turn, a mystery for the listener and reader to figure out how they did it. Each story is different, but each can be solved with careful listening and reading, and visualizing the story's events and images.

# 1.

## FISHING

One fine summer day two fathers and two sons went fishing at their favorite lake. They fished and talked all morning long and by noon everyone had caught one fish. As the two fathers and two sons walked back home, everyone was happy because each had a fish even though only three fish had been caught.

Two fathers and two sons. Only three fish and no fish were lost. How can this have happened?

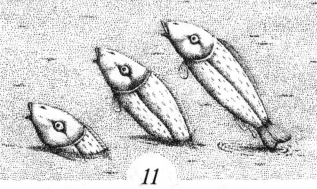

# HOW IT WAS DONE

Only three people went fishing.
A boy, his father, and his grandfather:
two sons and two fathers.

# 2.

# CROSSING THE RIVER

*O*nce there was a man who had to take a wolf, a goat, and a cabbage across a river. But his boat was so small it could hold only himself and one other thing. The man didn't know what to do. How could he take the wolf, the goat, and the cabbage over one at a time, so that the wolf wouldn't eat the goat and the goat wouldn't eat the cabbage?

# HOW IT WAS DONE

He could take the goat over

and go back alone.

Then take the wolf over

and then bring the goat back.

Then take the cabbage over and leave the goat behind.

And finally make one last trip

and take the goat over
to join the wolf and cabbage.

## Solution 2

He could take the goat over

and go back alone.

Then take the cabbage over

and bring the goat back.

Then take the wolf over and leave the goat behind.

And finally go back

and get the goat on the last trip.

*15*

# 3.

## TWO MOTHERS

Once in Tibet there lived a man who had two wives, but only the younger one had given birth to a son. To protect her son from the older jealous wife, the younger wife gave the boy to her to raise as her own. All went well until the father of the child died and the two wives began to fight as to who owned the house and who owned the boy who was to inherit everything. After much arguing the issue was finally taken to the king. Wanting to solve it as quickly as he could, the king called in both women and the boy.

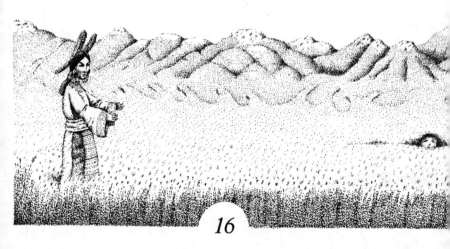

"As with all things," said the king to the two wives, "the stronger here shall win. The one of you that can hold fast to the boy shall hold him forever."

The king then had each woman take hold of one of the boy's arms and told them to pull. Instantly the boy cried out in pain and then found himself in a heap on the floor with the older wife.

"We have our proof," said the king, "of who the boy's true mother is. He shall live forever with the younger wife."

"But I pulled the harder," protested the older wife.

"Yes," said the king. "And you lost."

How did the king know the true mother of the boy?

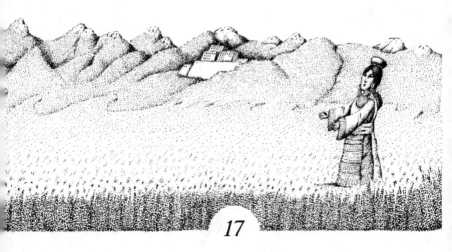

## HOW IT WAS DONE

The contest was not one of strength, but of love. The boy's true mother could not bear to hurt him and so she let go. She wanted him safe even if she could not be with him.

18

# 4.

## A DRINK FOR CROW

Once there was a crow who had grown so thirsty he could barely caw. He flew down to a big pitcher where he had gotten a drink of water the day before, but there was only a little bit of water remaining at the bottom. He tried and tried to reach it with his beak, but the pitcher was too deep and his beak was too short. But just as he was about to give up, he knew what to do. He flew back and forth from the garden to the pitcher until he was able to drink easily from the pitcher while sitting on its edge.

What did the crow do?

# HOW IT
# WAS DONE

The crow gathered pebbles,
one by one,
and dropped them
into the pitcher
until the water rose
to the top.

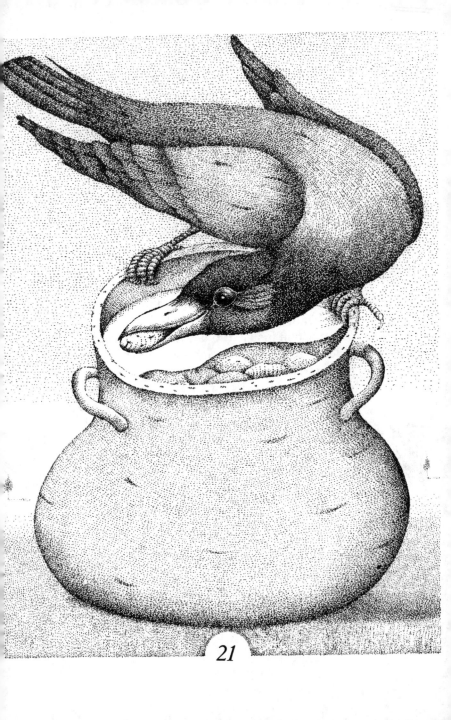

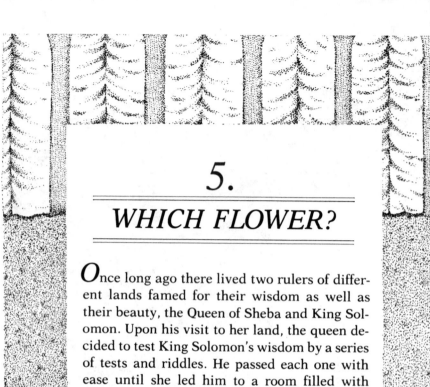

# 5.

## WHICH FLOWER?

$O$nce long ago there lived two rulers of different lands famed for their wisdom as well as their beauty, the Queen of Sheba and King Solomon. Upon his visit to her land, the queen decided to test King Solomon's wisdom by a series of tests and riddles. He passed each one with ease until she led him to a room filled with flowers of every shape and color. The queen had had the finest craftsmen and magicians in her land construct the flowers so that they looked exactly like the real flowers from her garden.

22

"The test," she told King Solomon, "is to find the ONE real flower amongst all the artificial ones."

King Solomon carefully looked from flower to flower and back again, searching for even the smallest of differences. He looked for any sign of wilted leaves or petals, but found lifelike leaves and petals in all conditions on every flower. And fragrance was of no help, for the room was filled with fragrances.

"Please," said King Solomon. "This room is so warm. Could we open the curtains and let in the breeze? The fresh air will clear my head for thinking."

The Queen of Sheba kindly agreed, and within minutes after the curtains had been opened King Solomon knew which of the many was the one real flower.

How did he suddenly know?

# HOW IT WAS DONE

A bee flew in the window
and immediately went
to the real flower.

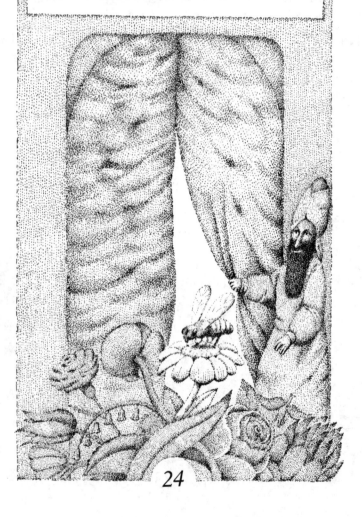

24

# 6.

## THE CLEVER BRIDE

*T*here was once a bride who lived with her mother-in-law and was very fond of chick peas. The bride liked them so much that she would steal some from the kitchen every day to roast and eat in secret. Before long, half the sack of chick peas was gone and the mother-in-law was angry.

She suspected the bride and mumbled to herself, "I'm certain she's the thief. She's the only new person in the house."

The mother-in-law was a smart woman, but the young bride was even cleverer. She knew she was being suspected.

One day, while cleaning house with her mother-in-law, the bride found a chick pea on the floor. She picked it up, showed it to her mother-in-law, and said three words that convinced the older woman that she hadn't taken the chick peas.

What did the bride say?

# HOW IT WAS DONE

"What is this?" If she did not know what a chick pea was, why would she steal it?

# 7.

## THE STICKS
## OF TRUTH

*L*ong ago in India judges traveled from village to village. One day a judge stopped at an inn to rest, but the innkeeper was very upset. Someone had just that day stolen his daughter's gold ring. The judge told him not to worry and had all the guests gather so that he could question them. When he could not figure out from their answers who the thief was, the judge decided to use some old magic. He told them all he was going to have to use the sticks of truth.

"These are magic sticks," he explained, "that will catch the thief."

He gave each guest a stick to keep under their bed during the night.

"The stick belonging to the thief will grow two inches during the night. At breakfast we will all compare sticks and the longest stick will be the thief's."

The next morning the judge had all the guests come by his table and hold their sticks up next to his to see if they had grown. But one after another all were the same. None of them had grown any longer. Then suddenly the judge called, "This is the thief! Her stick is shorter than all the rest."

Once caught, the woman confessed and the ring was returned. But all the guests were confused about the sticks of truth. The judge had said the longest stick would be the thief's, but instead it had been the shortest stick.

Why?

29

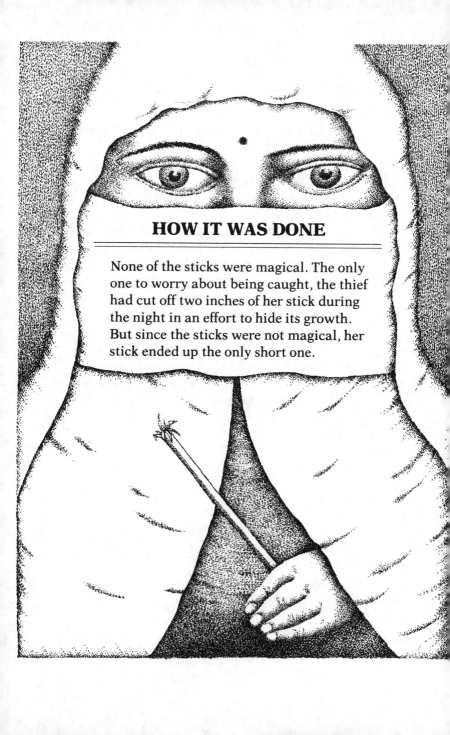

## HOW IT WAS DONE

None of the sticks were magical. The only one to worry about being caught, the thief had cut off two inches of her stick during the night in an effort to hide its growth. But since the sticks were not magical, her stick ended up the only short one.

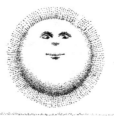

# 8.

## *THREE ROSEBUSHES*

$A$t one time the spirits came down into a village, took away three women, and turned them into three identical rosebushes in a field exactly alike in every way. Same color, fragrance, and shape. Same number of petals, leaves, and thorns. Except that one of the women had a husband and child. After much pleading, the spirits let her visit her family every night. Each night when the sun set, she would find herself at home; but as soon as the sun rose in the morning, she was again one of the three identical rosebushes in the

field. Still, she wanted to be with her family night and day as everyone does. She continued to listen to the spirits and one night told her husband, "Please. If you can do as I tell you, I will be able to be with you both night and day. Tomorrow once I leave, go to the field well before noon and look for three rosebushes exactly alike. If you can pick a rose from the bush that is me, I'll be set free."

When the sun began to rise, she was suddenly gone and back in the field. After tending the baby, but still well before noon, her husband went to the field and found three rosebushes exactly alike. He looked long and carefully, and he knew which one was his wife. He picked a rose from it and by the time he got back home his wife was there with the baby waiting for him.

How did he know which rosebush was his wife?

# HOW IT WAS DONE

Her rosebush had no dew
as did the other two
which had been out all night.

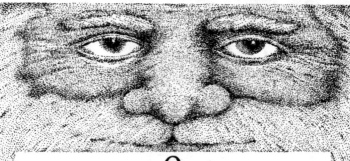

# 9.
## THE CLEVEREST SON

*O*nce there lived an old man who had three sons. When he grew old and ill and knew that he soon would die, he called all three sons into his room.

"There is no way I can divide the house and farm to support all three of you. The one who proves himself the cleverest will inherit the house and farm. There is a coin on the table for each of you. The one who can buy something that will fill this room will inherit all I own."

The eldest son took his coin, went straight to the marketplace, and filled his wagon full of straw. The second son thought a bit longer, then also went to the marketplace, where he bought sacks and sacks of feathers. The youngest son thought and then quietly went to a little shop. He bought two small things and tucked them into his pocket.

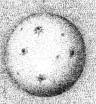

That night the father called them in to show what they had bought. The eldest son spread his straw about the floor, but it filled only one part of the room. The second son dumped out his sacks of feathers, but they filled only two corners of the room. Then the youngest son smiled, pulled the two small things out of his pocket, and soon filled the room.

"Yes," said the father, "you are indeed the cleverest and have filled my room when the others could not. You shall inherit my house and farm."

What had the youngest son bought and with what did he fill the room?

## HOW IT
## WAS DONE

A match and a candle that
filled the room with light.

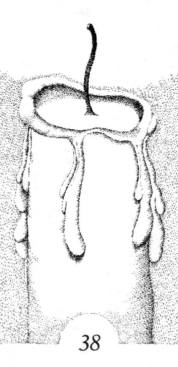

# 10.
## WORKING THE FIELD

Yasohachi worked as a farmer on a rich man's land. One spring the landlord came by and told all his farmers to get busy and smooth out the land in their care. Yasohachi's land was full of clumps and stones, but instead of working in the field he went home to rest. Day after day the landlord threatened him, but always Yasohachi just went home to rest. Then one day when the landlord was in the village he noticed people talking about a newly posted sign that read:

COME TO MY FIELD ON SUNDAY AFTERNOON AND WATCH ME CLIMB TO HEAVEN ON A BAMBOO POLE.

*Yasohachi*

The landlord was furious. He went straight to Yasohachi and said, "You can't get to heaven on a bamboo pole. Now get busy and get to work."

"I will," said Yasohachi. "But I have other things I have to do." And he went home and rested.

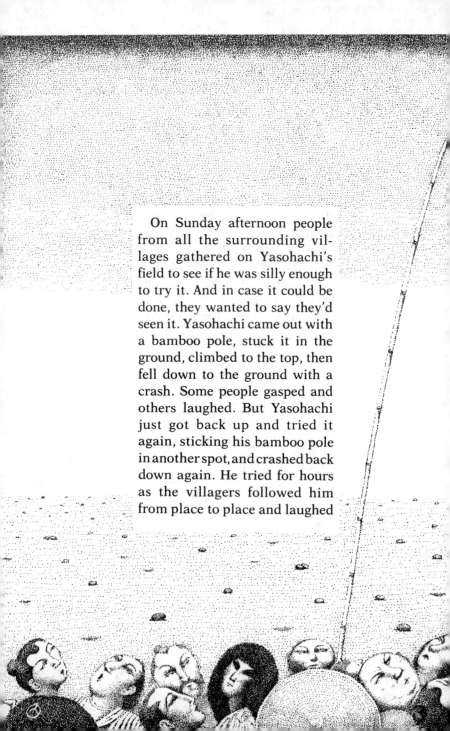

On Sunday afternoon people
from all the surrounding vil-
lages gathered on Yasohachi's
field to see if he was silly enough
to try it. And in case it could be
done, they wanted to say they'd
seen it. Yasohachi came out with
a bamboo pole, stuck it in the
ground, climbed to the top, then
fell down to the ground with a
crash. Some people gasped and
others laughed. But Yasohachi
just got back up and tried it
again, sticking his bamboo pole
in another spot, and crashed back
down again. He tried for hours
as the villagers followed him
from place to place and laughed

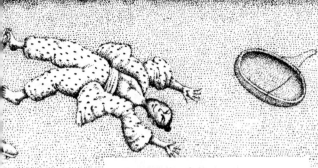

each time he fell.

But after a while people began to leave convinced he could never do it. By evening only the landlord and Yasohachi were left in the field.

"Now get busy and smooth out this land," yelled the landlord. "Or you won't be working for me anymore."

"Don't worry," Yasohachi said, dusting off his clothes. "My work is done. Just look for yourself."

And it was. Yasohachi's field was smooth and free of clods. He hadn't done his work, yet it had gotten done. How?

## HOW IT WAS DONE

All the people watching and following
him around the field with their
shuffling feet had smoothed out the
land and stomped out the clods of dirt.
Those who laughed at him had also
done his work for him.

# 11.

## THE GUILTY STONE

One day as he was walking near the edge of town, a judge saw a little boy crying at the side of the road.

"What's wrong?" asked the judge.

"I've been selling pastries all day long and someone has stolen my money," cried the boy. "I was so tired I put the money in my basket under the last of the pastries while I took a

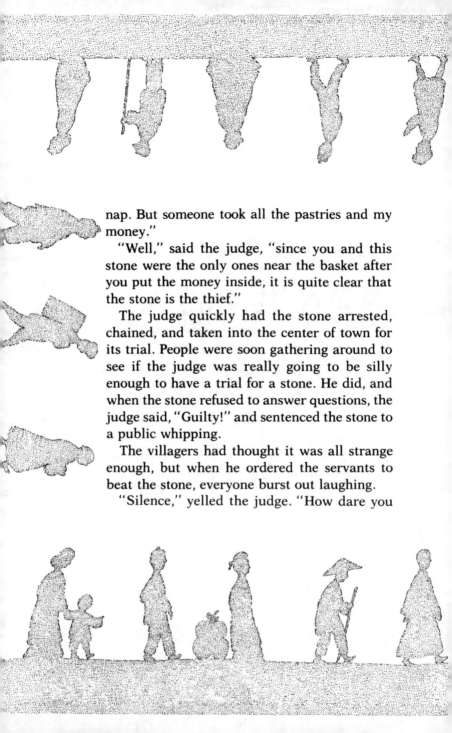

nap. But someone took all the pastries and my money."

"Well," said the judge, "since you and this stone were the only ones near the basket after you put the money inside, it is quite clear that the stone is the thief."

The judge quickly had the stone arrested, chained, and taken into the center of town for its trial. People were soon gathering around to see if the judge was really going to be silly enough to have a trial for a stone. He did, and when the stone refused to answer questions, the judge said, "Guilty!" and sentenced the stone to a public whipping.

The villagers had thought it was all strange enough, but when he ordered the servants to beat the stone, everyone burst out laughing.

"Silence," yelled the judge. "How dare you

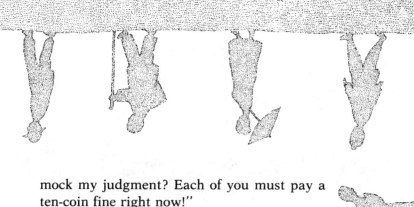

mock my judgment? Each of you must pay a ten-coin fine right now!"

As people searched their pockets for coins, the judge had a big jar of water brought near his chair.

"File by and drop your money into the jar," he ordered.

Being nervous for fear he might increase the fine if they laughed again, people quickly filed by, dropping their coins into the jar of water.

Suddenly the judge said, "This man is the real thief. Arrest him!"

Once caught, the man confessed and was taken off to jail. The people went home and the judge gave the boy all the coins in the jar to replace what the thief had stolen. Everyone was happy, but no one could figure out how the judge had discovered the thief. Can you?

## HOW IT WAS DONE

The thief's coins were those he had stolen
from the bottom of the greasy pastry
basket. When his coins were dropped into
the jar of water, bits of grease and frosting
floated to the surface.

# 12.

## DIVIDING THE HORSES

*O*nce there lived a farmer, his wife, and their three sons. When the farmer died, his will said that the eldest son was to receive one-half of what he owned, the middle son was to receive one-third, and the youngest son was to receive one-ninth. All the farmer owned, however, was seventeen horses. And try as they might, the three sons could not figure out any way to divide the seventeen horses by their father's wishes.

"Don't worry," their mother told them. "We can solve this with a little help."

She went to the neighboring farm and borrowed a horse. Then with a total of eighteen horses, she gave the eldest son one-half, or nine horses. She gave the middle son one-third, or six of the horses. And she gave the youngest son one-ninth, or two of the horses.

"There," she said. "Nine plus six plus two makes the seventeen horses your father left you." And she returned the eighteenth horse to the neighbor.

How did she do it?

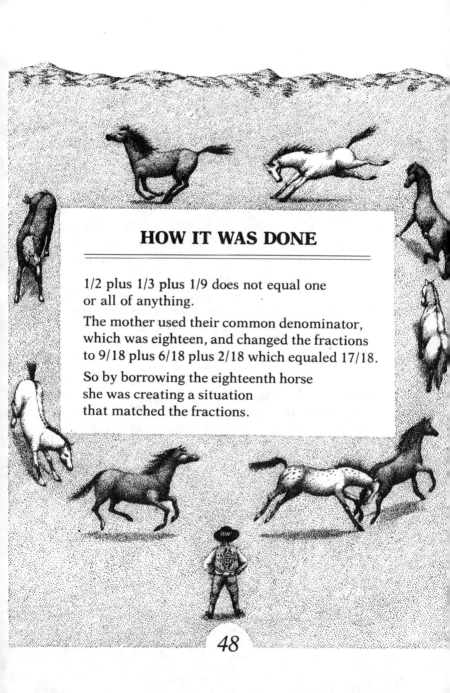

# HOW IT WAS DONE

1/2 plus 1/3 plus 1/9 does not equal one
or all of anything.

The mother used their common denominator,
which was eighteen, and changed the fractions
to 9/18 plus 6/18 plus 2/18 which equaled 17/18.

So by borrowing the eighteenth horse
she was creating a situation
that matched the fractions.

# 13.

## ONE WORD
## SOLVES A MYSTERY

*A* local merchant was preparing to go on a
selling trip. After loading his boat, he waited on
board for his servant. Seeing the merchant
waiting alone, the boatman decided it would
be easy to kill him and steal his goods. The
boatman quickly attacked and drowned the
merchant and took the goods to his own house.
And then to create an alibi, he went to the merchant's house and asked why he had not come
to the boat.

The merchant's wife had all her servants go

looking, but they could find no trace of him. In time the investigation reached the magistrate, who sent everyone out of the room except the merchant's wife. He asked her for an exact description of events at the time that the boatman first came to ask about her husband.

"My husband had already been gone quite a while," said the wife, "when the boatman came to our gate and called, 'Mistress, why hasn't the master come down yet?' "

Next the magistrate talked with the boatman who repeated exactly what he had said when he went to the merchant's house.

"That's it!" the magistrate told the boatman. "The merchant was killed and you are the killer. You just confessed."

"What confession?" protested the boatman.

Do you know what confession?

51

# HOW IT WAS DONE

When he came to the merchant's house, he called only for the mistress. He called for her because he knew, having killed the merchant, that he wasn't there.

# 14.

## HEAVEN AND HELL

*P*eople are always wishing. But once in China a man got his wish, which was to see the difference between heaven and hell before he died. When he visited hell, he saw tables crowded with delicious food, but everyone was hungry and angry. They had food, but were forced to sit several feet from the table and use chopsticks three feet long that made it impossible to get any food into their mouths.

When the man saw heaven, he was very surprised for it looked the same. Big tables of delicious food. People forced to sit several feet from the table and use three-foot long chopsticks that made it impossible to get any food into their mouths. It was exactly like hell, but in heaven the people were well fed and happy.

Why?

# HOW IT WAS DONE

In heaven they were feeding one another.

# *NOTES*

*1.* FISHING is a United States folktale retold from *Folklore from the Working Folk of America*, edited by Tristam P. Coffin and Hennig Cohen (Doubleday, 1974).

*2.* CROSSING THE RIVER is a world-wide tale. This variant is retold from "Wolf, Goat, and Cabbage" in *Noodles, Nitwits, and Numskulls*, edited by Maria Leach (World Publishing Co., 1961). An African Hausa variant can be found in *African Folktales*, edited by Roger D. Abrahams (Pantheon, 1983).

*3.* TWO MOTHERS is retold from *Tibetan Tales* by F. Anton V. Schiefner (London: George Routledge, 1906). It is a variant of the well-known King Solomon tale of threatening to cut the baby in half.

*4.* A DRINK FOR CROW is one of the Aesop fables and is found in endless collections.

*5.* WHICH FLOWER? is one of the King Solomon stories and is retold from various sources, including *Favorite Stories Old and New*, rev. ed., edited by Sidonie M. Gruenberg (Doubleday, 1955) and *The Wisest Man in the World* by Benjamin Elkin (Parents Magazine Press, 1968).

*6.* THE CLEVER BRIDE is retold from "Chick-Peas" in *Apples of Immortality: Folktales of Armenia*, edited by Leon Surmelian (University of California Press, 1968).

*56*

*7.* THE STICKS OF TRUTH is retold from "Folklore of Chitral" by J. Davidson, *Indian Antiquary, XXIX* (Bombay, September 1900).

*8.* THREE ROSEBUSHES is one of the stories collected by the Brothers Grimm.

*9.* THE CLEVEREST SON is an Ethiopian tale retold from *Unicef Book of Children's Legends*, compiled by William I. Kaufman (Stackpole Books, 1970).

*10.* WORKING THE FIELD is retold from "Yasohachi and Heaven" in *Men from the Village Deep in the Mountains and Other Japanese Folk Tales*, translated by Garrett Bang (Macmillan, 1973).

*11.* THE GUILTY STONE is an Asian tale retold from several sources, including *The Magic Spear and Other Stories of China's Famous Heroes* by Louise Crane (Random House, 1938) and *Pebbles from a Broken Jar* by Frances Alexander (Bobbs-Merrill, 1969).

*12.* I first heard DIVIDING THE HORSES in 1982 from my father, David W. Shannon, a math teacher, who did not know how long he had known the story. Variants can be found in *A Treasury of Jewish Folklore*, edited by Nathan Ausubel (Crown, 1948) and *Eurasian Folk and Fairy Tales* by I. F. Bulatkin (Criterion Books, 1965).

*13.* ONE WORD SOLVES A MYSTERY is retold from *Chinese Fairy Tales and Fantasies*, edited by Moss Roberts (Pantheon, 1979).

*14.* HEAVEN AND HELL is retold from *Tales from Old China* by Isabelle C. Chang (Random House, 1969) and *Studies in Jewish and World Folklore* by Haim Schwarzbaum (Berlin: Walter De Gruyter & Co., 1968).